T0365969

STANDING
A
L
O
N
E

PAUL JONES

Order this book online at www.trafford.com
or email orders@trafford.com

Most Trafford titles are also available at major online book retailers.

Print information available on the last page.

ISBN: 978-1-6987-0650-4 (sc)
ISBN: 978-1-6987-0652-8 (hc)
ISBN: 978-1-6987-0651-1 (e)

Library of Congress Control Number: 2021905296

Trafford rev. 03/12/2021

 www.trafford.com
North America & international
toll-free: 844-688-6899 (USA & Canada)
fax: 812 355 4082

Saving Souls

We all have those moments in our lives when we need reassurance, or we might just want to break down and have a good cry.

Standing Alone is a book of poetry that is meant to inspire and touch the living soul, poems such as "Standing Alone"

and "There for Me." Both poems may have the same conclusion, but doing the process, one will reach that conclusion in our own special way.

Contents

Be strong and courageous. Do not fear or be in dread of them, for it is you the LORD your God who goes with you. He will not leave you or forsake.

—Deuteronomy 31:6 ESV

Standing Alone

As I walk through the valley of shadows of death,
As I pass by a mirror, I stopped and took a good look at myself.
I felt as if I was all alone.
Right then and there, I wanted to go home.
I heard a voice coming from deep inside.
I wanted to run, I wanted to hide.
I looked around, and as far as I could see,
There was no one else there besides me.
The voice told me not to be afraid or not to fear.
Because If you knew who it was, you would be full of cheer.
I asked, "Through all of my hard times, why have you forsaken me?"
Because it was during those times I was by myself as far as I could see.

He didn't say another word. He just let me talk.
I wanted to leave, I wanted to run, but I couldn't even walk.
And then I took a look back over my years.
I looked at the times that I had shed many tears.
I looked at the times that I did things that I shouldn't have done.
All because they made me feel good and I thought that they were fun;
All the times that I thought that I couldn't make it,
All the times that I wanted to just give up and quit.
And then I thought—and I fell down on my knee—
It was you, you, Lord, you were the one that saved me.
I thought to myself, your love and your grace I do not deserve.
But yet it's me that you continue to serve.
Why do you do so much for me?

Is there something in me that I don't see?
He told me to get up and go.
He said that when the time is right, then you will know.
I was able to open my eyes and stand up.
I no longer felt like I was stuck.
As I started to dry my eyes and walk away,
He said, "All I ask you to do is continue to pray."
And from that very day and on,
I knew that I would never have to stand alone.

For God so loved the world, that he gave his only Son, that whoever believes in him should not perish but have eternal life. For God did not send his Son into the world to condemn the world, but in order that the world might be saved through him.

—John 3:16–17 ESV

Where Would I Be

I can only imagine where I would be
If my Lord wasn't willing to die upon that tree.
They nailed Him up there, all stretched out wide,
While all of the time, he was thinking of me deep down inside.
And then His blood started to drop.
But you know, that if He wanted to, He could have made it stop.
And then He died, and for the world to know,
The heavens itself put on a show.
But yet his love for me still wasn't finished.
He still had to go into hell to show satan
that his powers over death were diminished.
I think back, if He had not done this for me,
Only He knows where I would be.

When most think of love, they might
think of Cupid or little turtle doves.
But He gave up His life for me, now that is love.
When I think of my Lord, all stretch out wide,
I get a special feeling deep down inside.
I know that He didn't do this just for me.
He did this so we can all might become His family.

You were bought with a price. So, glorify God in your body.
—1 Corinthians 6:20 ESV

Spreading His Love

I ran to the hall and then across the floor.
And then I forced open the old wooden door.
They said he was down the hall and to the right.
I knew, if found him, I wouldn't let him out of my sight.
And then I passed a mirror, and what did I see?
I saw Him, and He was on the inside of me.
I asked Him, "How long have you been there?"
He answered, "I've been here before your first breath of air."
I asked Him, "How long do you plan to stay?"
He said, "Oh, I'll be here until you pass away."
And then I saw two birds fly, they were two doves.
He said, "I chose you to help spread my message of love."

I had to ask, "Why would you choose me?"
He answered, "There's a lot in you, a lot you can't yet see."
"How would I know where to start? How
would I know when the time is right?"
He said, "I just want you to get a pen and paper and start to write."
The words that I put on paper, they started to flow.
Where are these words coming from, I don't know.
He told me to write on every subject matter.
To some, it will be the gospel, and some
others, they would run and scatter.
To some, it will come as a relief, and to others, it will test their belief.
But overall, I want you to share my message of love because
with me and my Father, that's all it's about up here above.

Peace I leave with you; my peace I give to you. Not as the world gives do I give to you. Let not your hearts be troubled, neither let them be afraid.

—John 14:27 ESV

The Peace Within

When I'm with you, there's nothing but peace.
My worries in this world are the least.
Even when I don't see you,
you are always by my side
because I know that for me, you hung
on that cross and died.
Because of the blood you shed,
I will never have to steal, borrow, or beg.
I know that when it's all over,
and from this earth I'm gone,
that you've already prepared a place for me, a new home.
My age, I will never have to worry,
I will never grow old,
and the streets that I walk on will be made of gold.

I know, as long as I'm in this life,
there will still be the pain, hurt, and strife.
For now, all of the worrying I have can cease
because my Lord lives so that I can have peace.

Keep your life free from love of money, and be content with what you have, for he has said, "I will never leave you nor forsake you."

—Hebrews 13:5 ESV

There for Me

As I walk through this land of pain and sorrow,
I wonder in my mind, will you be there for me again tomorrow?
Every day of my life, you have been there for me.
For what reason, I wonder, for what reason.
I guess I just have to wait and see.
The thoughts of you flow in and out of my head.
I wonder if there will be thoughts of you even when I'm dead.
As for now, when I lay down to sleep,
I find myself holding my pillow, and I began to weep.
I try so hard not to let my thoughts stray,
but yet I find myself doing this every day.

I know that my feet are planted on solid ground,
but yet the negative thoughts in my mind are still found.
But then there's still a smile on my face when I wake up and see
that you haven't left and you are still there for me.

For everyone who asks receives, and the one who seeks
finds, and to the one who knocks it will be opened.

—Matthew 7:8 ESV

Trapped Within

Doing the day, I sit in a room that's full of light.
But yet the room is still dark when it should be good and bright.
I feel like I've been placed inside of a box;
A box made of metal, a box that is locked.
I look for someone to help, but which way will they come?
I cried out loud, but yet there were still none.
I remembered what I was taught when I was young,
that was to look until the hills for there my help will come from.
I hold my head up, and I began to pray.
But I've been lost for so long, I don't know what to say.
All of a sudden, words started to come out.
They came out with such a flow, I wanted to shout.

And then all of a sudden, I was out of the box.
Not only did I begin to walk, I began to trot.
I then lifted up my voice to give Him praise.
There was no more darkness, there wasn't any more shade.
He told me not to wait until I can't see.
"You can always call on Me.
My voice you may not always hear.
But I can assure you that I'm always near."
He said that there's not a way for me to hide
because all you have to do is to look deep inside.
I turned my head, and I started to look.
And then my eyes landed on His book.
He said, "The words that are written within
will let you know that you will always have a friend.

Not only do you always have a friend in Me,
but I also welcome you into My family."
All of a sudden, out of my eye, a tear started to fall.
He said, "You don't have to cry, all you have to do is call.
But when you don't hear me, do not be deceived
because all you have to do is to believe.

Times might get hard, and they might get tough.
But I will carry you through all of those times that are rough.
Just think back over your years,
all of the times that you had shed many of tears.
I was there for your father and your mother.
I was there for your sister and your brother.
I told you this so you will know that My words are true
and so you will know that I will also be there for you."

Remember not the former things, nor consider the things of old.
—Isaiah 43:1 ESV

Looking Back

As I walk through this valley of shadows of death,
I try not to look back at my old self.
I try not to look back at the places that I've been
because behind me is a lot of trouble, a lot of sin.
Sometimes I didn't know where I would get a dinner plate.
And if I got home at all, I got home really late.
I can't begin to tell you of all of the tears that I've shed,
of all the times I've woke up in strange beds.
As a matter of fact, when I think of things that I've done,
I'm not surprised when they tell me that
I might have four or five sons.
But now I hold my head up high
as I look up into the sky.

All of a sudden, my heart starts to sing.
My soul is saved by the Almighty King.
He said, that if I wanted to change my way,
all I had to do was to lift my voice and pray.
Now I stand before you today,
and I can proudly say
that when I look in the mirror, at my face,
I know in my heart that I've been saved by His grace.

For since we believe that Jesus died and rose again, even so, through
Jesus, God will bring with him those who have fallen asleep.

—1 Thessalonians 4:14 ESV

Resurrection

I looked inside deep into the ground.
But yet my Lord's body was not found.
There was a deep fear that came over me.
I did not see whom I come to see.
I could not move, I could not stand.
I was met by this being that I thought was a man.
He asked why do I cry, why do I wipe.
I replied I did not find the one that I come to seek.
He told me there was no need to cry.
He told me to dry every tear from my eye.
He said, "The one that you seek is not here. He is gone.
He has ascended to His Father. He will not be there long."

Then he said to me, just as sure as my Lord was hung on a tree,
to go tell His disciples and Peter to meet Him in Galilee.
As two of the disciples walked along the way,
they met who they thought was a stranger
that walked with them that day.
After they told the rest, they did not believe.
They thought, in their hearts, they were being deceived.
He sat down with them as they ate meat.
Then they realized that this was He whom they seek.
He told them to go into the world and preach,
to preach the gospel to everyone they reached.
He then looked at His disciples, all eleven.
He smiled at them and then ascended into heaven.

For I know the plans I have for you, declares the LORD, plans for welfare and not for evil, to give you a future and a hope.

—Jeremiah 29:11

All You Have

There is only one true love,
which is the love that comes from above.
Jesus gave His life for us all
because He knew that we would stumble and fall.
From where does love come from,
and why does it come much easier for others than some?
We can say that we love each other,
but we can't even love our sisters and brothers.
So what is love, how can we know?
Why is it so easy to speak but yet so hard to show?
I can tell you that I love you,
but how do you know that my words are true?
I say that my love for you is as high as the sky,
but will I be willing to lay down my life and die?

Gifts and money, you might receive,
but is this a plot to get you to believe?
God gave His only begotten Son,
but yet we still ask, what is love? Are we truly dumb?

For by grace, you have the gift of God, not a result of works, so that no one may boast. been saved through faith. And this is not your own doing; it is

—Ephesians 2:8–9 ESV

Anew

Oh, how can it be true,
each morning we wake up, we are born anew.
Just like when a horse runs his race,
the steps in our lives we can't erase.
But it's up to us to do the things that we were chose to do
To walk in our lives the lives that are true
Every morning we wake up, the sun will shine.
The things that were the day before, we should leave behind.
But you think about the things you've done in lust.
The thoughts in your head, should you really trust?
When you look in the mirror, you look deeper than a glance.
Seeing this, you know that you're given another chance.

Thinking about the things you may have done the night before,
but knowing who you are born of, you quickly shut that door.
You stop feeling sorry for yourself, and your head you raise.
Then you open up your mouth, and you give Him all of the praise.

Yet you do not know what tomorrow will bring. What is your life?
For you are a mist that appears for a little time and then vanishes.
—James 4:14 ESV

One Voice

I hear the thunder, and I see the rain.
I feel so much hurt, I feel so much pain.
Which direction should I go? Which direction am I led?
Who do I listen to, which voice that's in my head?
One voice tells me that I should live my life right.
And one tells me I don't have to fight.
One voice keeps telling me I'm not good enough to receive.
But the other voice keeps telling me all I have to do is to believe.
One voice says that I have to run in this life to keep pace.
But the other voice says that all I have to do is to rest in His grace.
One voice keeps telling me I must do all that I can to be the man.

But the other voice says, on His word, all I have to do is to stand.
One voice keeps telling me I can end it all with a knife.
But the other voice says, "I have taken care of it all with My life."

Behold, I stand at the door and knock. If anyone
hears my voice and opens the door, I will come in
to him and eat with him, and he with me.

—Revelation 3:20 ESV

Listening for His Voice

He waits for you with opened arms.
Know in your heart that it wasn't
Him which caused the harm.
You asked the Lord, "Why did I have to fall?"
He answered, "When I tried to help, you wouldn't
open your heart, you wouldn't answer My call."
I thought life was a struggle, I thought it was a game.
So losing my family, I thought, who was to blame?
He asked, "What do you regret the most
while living at such a fast pace
that you never took the time to receive and my grace?"
I thought, for the rest of my life, I would be all
alone and life would be such a bore.

It was at that moment that my family
walked back through the door.
My head and my hands I would raise.
Right then, I lifted my voice and gave Him praise.

For Christ also suffered once for sins, the righteous for the unrighteous, that he might bring us to God, being put to death in the flesh but made alive in the spirit.

—1 Peter 3:18 ESV

Resurrection Day

Asked to write a poem about resurrection day,
these are the words that I was instructed to say.
I never asked for you to celebrate this day.
But I should be deep in your hearts, in your hearts always.
The words that they speak of me are forever true.
I gave up my life for the love of each one of you.
Some may ask why did I go through so
much pain and embarrassment.
But I knew that this would happen before I was sent.
They wanted me to walk in humiliation.
They wanted me to walk in shame.
Even the one that walked with me pretended
to not even know my name.

Some might think that I could have taken
the thirty-nine stripes with ease.
No, I took them this way so that there would
be a cure for all of mankind disease.
I received the crown of thorns on my head and torment of my brain
so that all my people can live a full life and not walk around insane.
I carried my own cross upon my weary shoulders
so that my people can walk through their
lives not tired and bent over.
I hung on my cross all stretched out wide
so that I could receive my people sins deep
down in me, deep down inside.
When I died and went into hell, satan himself
thought that it was finished.

But he didn't know that I did this so
that his power over death would be diminished.
I was raised back up on the third day
so that my people, who believe, will know that
none of them in hell will have to stay.
So on this day, if you choose to celebrate,
do it in knowing that because of my death, you will
have a chance to walk through those gates.

And the devil who had deceived them was thrown into the lake of fire and sulfur where the beast and the false prophet were, and they will be tormented day and night forever and ever.

—Revelation 20:10 ESV

The Beat Down

Now I believe that when Jesus died and went down to hades,
Old satan wheeled in, in his fiery old burned-up Mercedes.
He called his minions, from the north, south, east, and west gates.
He said, "Come on, y'all, let's celebrate."
But Jesus opened his eyes, and then He began to speak.
He told them, "I won't even be here for a week."
Old satan looked around, and he told Him, "You're in
my place now, what can you do?"
Jesus said, "I suggest that you turn around and look behind you."
Old satan thought that He was bluffing at first,
but he slowly turned around,
and when he did, he saw that all of his minions had hit the ground.
"So this is why you came here, this is why you were sent."
"Yes, for this reason, but my Father was
hoping that you would repent."
"So the words that they speak of Your Father are still true."
"Yes, my Father is the one that never gives up on you."
Old satan said, "Before it's over, I will be the one,
I will be the one laughing and having all of the fun."
Jesus said, "I knew those were the words that you would say,
so the power that you have over my people ends today.
The only thing that you can do is to whisper into their ear,
but My Holy Spirit will dull your voice so
that you won't be very clear."

Jesus turned around and saw His saints of old.
He told them to "come on with Me so that you can be clothed."
Old satan looked at Him and said, "So my
power over death is finished."
Jesus replied, "Yes, your power over death is now diminished."
On the third day, Jesus started to ascend.
Old satan tried to stop Him, but he knew that this was his end.

In the beginning was the Word, and the Word
was with God, and the Word was God.

—John 1:1 ESV

The Beginning

The wind blew such a bitterly cold,
the type that would cut you deep, deep down into your soul.
Not a star was in the sky, it wasn't very bright.
Even satan himself couldn't see because there wasn't any light.
It was just one big rock floating around in the sky.
But yet still, it caught His very eye.
Yet there was no light, not even a trace,
until God decided to show up Himself and show His face.
He then saw the waters, and He developed His plan.
He separated the waters so there could be dry land.
The dirt on the earth was made rich indeed
so that the grass and plants could grow from their very own seeds.

In the sky, He put the moon by night,
but for the day was the sun, giving off heat, big and bright.
Then He put the fish and creatures in the sea
and then all the creatures on land, down to the smallest bee,
so that the creatures would live and not die.
He told them to be fruitful and to multiply.
He then looked at the earth, he looked at the land,
and then He said, "In our image, let us make man.
Once again, I have done my best.
And now, as I look over all my doings, I shall simply rest."

Then I saw a new heaven and a new earth, for the first heaven and the first earth had passed away, and the sea was no more.

—Revelation 21:1 ESV

Wondering Soul

This morning, when I woke up, I really wondered.
I saw the clouds, and I heard the thunder.
I got up, and I walked around my room.
It was so cold and dark, it was filled with gloom.
I turned and looked at my bed. What did I see?
It was a silhouette, and it looked just like me.
I thought to myself, am I being deceived?
What is this? What should I really believe?
I continued on doing the things I had to do.
I wondered what was for real, what was really true.
I shook my head to get the cobwebs out.
All of a sudden, I heard a loud shout.
I wondered, who this could be?
For there was no one else there besides me.
I wondered, I had no clue.

I wanted to leave, I did not know what to do.
I tried to turn my head, tried to shut my eyes,
but it was just like "Sherlock Holmes." It was like little spies.
The more I tried to run, the more I tried to hide.
Eventually, I came to the conclusion that I have died.
I looked around to see all that I could see,
but all I could see was darkness looking back at me.
All of a sudden, a light started to shine.
Was I going to heaven, or was I going to be left behind?
I tried to think back about all the things I used to do,
but I still did not know, I didn't have a clue.
I heard a voice asking, "Do you deserve this, son?
Why don't you tell me all of the things you've done?"
I did not know what to do, I did not know what to say.
I wanted to tell the truth and not let my answers stray.
I remembered some of the evil things that I had done,
all in the name of lust, all in the name of fun.
I slowly held my head down to the ground
and thought that I was hell-bound.
When I looked up, I saw the opened gates.

I didn't know what to think, it had to be a mistake.
As I walked in, I was greeted with a smile.
I heard a voice say, "Come on in, you have
walked some long hard miles."
When I walked in, I saw all the beauty there could possibly be.
I saw all the beauty that anyone could hope to see.

But if asked what did it look like,
it was if I lost my sight.
To speak of a beautiful place is simply untold.
You will just have to wait to discover the place for your soul.

Since you have been born again, not of perishable seed but of imperishable, through the living and abiding word of God.

—1 Peter 1:23 ESV

The Seed

On the earth, He placed His mighty hand,
and from that touch was made the very first man.
And with that, man was laid, a great foundation,
one that was laid and developed into many nations.
And in each man was planted a seed.
But does a plant grow without any weeds?
All He asked was that His commandment we keep.
There would not have been any tears for us to weep.
But even with only two,
we found that so hard to do.
We did not try to repent,
but he blamed it on the help that was sent.
From that point, he let it in.

He opened his arms and welcomed sin.
From that sin was planted a curse.
Passing through generation, the curse grew worse,
from lying to stealing, to killing.
When will it stop? When will we start the healing?
Plants find it very hard to grow.
When will the healing start, does anyone know?
Many say that they believe.
Do they really, or are they once again tying to deceive?

Is anyone among you suffering? Let him pray. Is anyone cheerful? Let him sing praise.

—James 5:13

Music

We all listen to the music we choose.
It doesn't matter if it's spiritual, gospel, or blues.
We all know Jesus can work it out,
which is enough to make us all want to scream and shout.
Then we have. I never would have made it,
which is enough to keep us going,. to not let us quit
Before the rap songs came, that make us want to fight,
it was the happy-go-lucky for our enjoyment, Rapper Delight.
And then we have songs to make you think
that it's only for the lonely,
but I'm here to tell you that the words are true, that
the kingdom of God is for members only.
There is no need to worry, ponder, or stress
because anyone can join, all you have to do is to believe and confess.
The Lord says to us to come one and all.
You don't have to be lonely, chosen, or called.
When you feel like all you had and loved is gone and departed,
you can turn to Him even if you are
brokenhearted.
If you don't have a dime and you can't pay,
you don't need any money, you can come anyway.

The saying is trustworthy: If anyone aspires to the office of overseer, he desires a noble task. Therefore, an overseer must be above reproach, the husband of one wife, sober-minded, self-controlled, respectable, hospitable, able to teach, not a drunkard, not violent but gentle, not quarrelsome, not a lover of money. He must manage his own household well, with all dignity keeping his children submissive, for if someone does not know how to manage his own household, how will he care for God's church?

—1 Timothy 3:1–16

Saving Souls

Old satan and I used to walk hand in hand.
I once thought he was my friend, that he was the man.
He kept me out all night long, and I thought that it was fun.
He kept me out until the break of dawn.
But one day I felt really bad, and I wanted to end it all.
That is when Christ appeared to me, and
somehow I knew that I was called.
I thought that I would be called only to teach,
but He said, "No, I called you not only to teach, but also to preach."
A preacher, I didn't want to be. All I wanted to do was to teach
because being a preacher, I would have to be a shepherd to His sheep.

I complained until the day that I was shown my own heart.
That was the day that I knew that I would have to start.
Lord, where will I go? What will I say?
He said not to worry but for me to walk this way.
Now, until this very day, I love what I do,
and I came to discover that I love His people too.

Have I not commanded you? Be strong and courageous.
Do not be frightened, and do not be dismayed, for the
LORD your God is with you wherever you go.

—Joshua 1:9 ESV

All by Myself

At times you might feel like you're alone,
although you have a family, you have a home.
You feel like you're all by yourself.
You feel like there is no one else.
There is no reason nor anyone to blame,
But from time to time, things just doesn't feel the same.
Some negative thoughts might come into your head,
thoughts that might make you think that you're better off dead.
And then a voice on the inside starts to speak.
The voice tells you not to give in, not to be weak.
He tells you, "I have a purpose for your life,
and it's not only for your children and your wife."

He said, "I want you to share with others what I have given you,
the words that I give you, the words that are true."
He said, "The thoughts that come to your
head and make you want to stray,
they come to you to stop you from saying
the things that I want you to say.
So when you're feeling lonely and feeling like there's no one else,
I'm here to tell you that you're never by yourself."

But you, O Lord, are a God merciful and gracious, slow to anger and abounding in steadfast love and faithfulness.

—Psalm 86:15 ESV

Just His Love

When I look around, and I see the morning dew,
I can say that the love You have for me is purely true.
When I wake up and take my morning breath,
I know that the love You have for me is righteousness.
And for that reason, I don't have to second-guess.
With the love You have for me,
I can open my eyes, and from this world, I can clearly see.
My Lord gives me more love than I truly deserve.
And for that reason, it's me that He continues to serve.
When I make a mistake and fall down,
my Lord picks me up, and with His love, He surrounds.

When I was a sinner, and I never fail down on my knee,
it was because of His love, that my Lord yet died for me.
So the love that I have in me
could never measure up to the love my
Lord has, the love that I now see.

In this is love, not that we have loved God but that he loved us and sent his Son to be the propitiation for our sins.
—1 John 4:10 ESV

His Message

Being saved by His grace is more than not going to hell.
Being saved by His grace often gives you a story to tell.
My Lord asks that we go out and spread His word,
the word that's in your heart, the word that you've just heard.
He wants us to spread His message of love,
the true love that He sent by His son from up above.
He doesn't want the message to come from our minds.
His message of love is not just made-up lines.
If you sit down and listen and open up your heart,
His message of love will soon come, it will soon start.

God so loved the world that He gave His only begotten Son.
Do you think He would have done this if His work was done?
The grace He has is given to every man, woman, and child.
So there is no excuse for us growing up wild.
He didn't want us to grow up like the rest.
He meant for us to grow up in loved and to be blessed.

Fear not, for I am with you; be not dismayed, for I
am your God; I will strengthen you, I will help you, I
will uphold you with my righteous right hand.

—Isaiah 41:10 ESV

Trying Too Hard

Lord, all of the words that I read about You, I know to be true.
But when it comes to them manifesting in my life,
sometimes it makes me wonder, sometimes I have thought twice.
Your words say, "I can do all things through
Christ who strengthens me,"
but sometimes in this world, those things are hard to see.
Your word says to trust in the Lord with all of my heart,
but sometimes in this world, I wonder, how do I start?
Your word says give and it shall be given back to me,
but when my pockets are empty, that becomes too hard see.

Once again, Lord, I know that the words
that I read about you are true.
Oh, now I believe, I see.
I've been trying to do everything through me.
It's when I sit back and take my hands off,
It's then I come to the realization that You've already paid the cost.
It's then that I don't have look for things nor think twice,
that you're the one that causes things to manifest in my life.

Do not be anxious about anything, but in everything
by prayer and supplication with thanksgiving let
your requests be made known to God.

—Philippians 4:6 ESV

Just Be Still

Lord, when I think back over all of my years,
and all you ever wanted me to do is to trust in You and be still.
Not that You didn't want me to do anything or to not move,
even when I did do those things that You might not have approved,
You still put Your hand out before me and led my way
Because You knew that the direction that
I was going, I wasn't going to stay.
Even now, when my mind gets to wondering
and the thoughts won't cease,
You're the one to calm me down and to give me peace.
Lord, I know that Your word is true and You are for real,
so why is it so hard for me to just trust in You and just be still?
Even now, as I pray and meditate on your word,
my mind often wonders, are my prayers being heard?
But then I look back over my years,
those years that You worked on me and
dried away my tears.
And now I see that Your work on me wasn't a waste,
but I still must practice the patience that You
placed in me and not be in such a haste.

The Lord is not slow to fulfill his promise as some coun2
t slowness, but is patient toward you, not wishing that any
should perish, but that all should reach repentance.

— **Peter 3:9** ESV

No Remorse

As I walk through the valley of shadows of death,
I truly feel in my heart I have nothing left.
I feel like I've done all that I could,
and it doesn't matter if it was bad or if it was good.
They say that my Lord died for me.
I guess I should just open my eyes so that I can see.
They say that I was all part of His plan,
that all I have to do is to believe in Him and take a stand.
Sometimes I feel like a tree blowing in the wind.
Is there still hope for me, or is there just sin?
They say that if I confess in Him, I'll receive His grace.
So how come at times I still feel out of place?

They say that if you go down your knees and confess His name,
things in your life will never be the same.
But now, since I done this and I can see,
can someone please tell me, why does satan comes for me?
Is it because, in my heart and mind, I expect more?
It's like trying to fit my hopes and dreams through a narrow door.
Old satan says, "If you turn from Him and follow me,
I will widen that door for you, you will see."
But I will not turn away—I will follow my Lord's course
because then, in my heart, I will know that there will be no remorse.

A Song of Ascents. I lift up my eyes to the hills. From where does my help come? My help comes from the LORD, who made heaven and earth. He will not let your foot be moved; he who keeps you will not slumber. Behold, he who keeps Israel will neither slumber nor sleep. The LORD is your keeper; the LORD is your shade on your right hand . . .

—Psalm 121:1–8 ESV

Looking Toward The Hills

As I walk through the valley of shadow of death,
I think my feelings are all that I have left.
I started to live off of my emotions,
but all that did was to cause a lot of commotion.
I had to find a way to get my life back right,
but it wasn't something I could see, it wasn't within my sight.
Why couldn't I find help? Why couldn't I see?
Was the help I was looking for just avoiding me?
I searched for my help, I looked high and low.
Where will my help come from, I don't know?
I first thought that my help came from drugs and pills,
but then I remembered that I must look toward the hill.

Looking toward the hill, what does this mean?
I looked toward the hill, but yet there was no help seen.
But then I remembered that my Lord died on a hill upon a cross,
and He did this so that my soul wouldn't be lost.
This was the help that I was looking for.
My help came to me just as soon as I opened my heart's door.

....

And this is eternal life, that they know you the only
true God, and Jesus Christ whom you have sent.

—John 17:3 ESV

I Never Knew

I never knew my Lord like this before.
I ran to Him, and He opened many of doors.
He opened my eyes, and the sun rose and shined.
I ran to him, and He gave me peace of mind.
He told me that He gave His love for me,
and all I had to do was to open my heart to see.
He's given me all things according to His will,
and all He asks in return is for me to trust in Him and be still.
I never knew of a real true love
until He sent His son down here from above.
Jesus gave up His life for me
so that none of the negative things has to be.
And now I walk around with a smile on my face
because I do know that I'm saved by His grace.

Therefore, if anyone is in Christ, he is a new creation.
The old has passed away; behold, the new has come.

—2 Corinthians 5:17 ESV

Breaking Free

Break free from the chains of the past.
You're the one helping them to last.
They say to trust in the Lord with all of your heart.
When will you begin? When will you start?
You think about the things that you used to do.
You often think about them because they felt good to you.
Sometimes you feel like you're all alone.
You feel like you need to call your past up on the phone,
even though your past didn't go the way you wanted it to go,
But your past is all that you really know.
Your past provided you a false sense of security.

Even though your past was worse than your
present reality,
could this be because we know what was behind us?
And for our future, we find it so hard in Him to trust.
We stand in one place; we try to look down the road.
We want to know what's ahead; we want to be told.
Even the children of Israel, who was being led to a new home,
all they could ever do was to look back, complain, and moan.
So when it looks like you're all alone,
Just call on Him and put down that phone.
Your future might not be what you think it will be,
but to find out, you let go of the past, you must learn to break free.

For "everyone who calls on the name of the Lord will be saved."
—Romans 10:13 ESV

Seeing in The Dark

When your future looks dull and you can't see,
that's when our Lord says, "Call on Me."
We often want to turn to everyone else.
Some of us even try to solve our problems all by ourselves.
We often forget to reach out and take His hand.
We forget that we're all part of His righteous plan.
We start to search for answers within our minds.
We think that the answer is there and easy to find.
So when your future is dull and it seems out of your sight,
it can be fixed simply by just turning on His light.

All Scripture is breathed out by God and profitable for teaching, for reproof, for correction, and for training in righteousness.
—2 Timothy 3:16 ESV

His Words

Listen to the words that come out of His mouth.
You cannot tell if He's from the north or south.
His letters are not capital or bold,
but they pierce deep, deep down into the soul.
Those words, how did He learn to speak?
His words, they reach you even when you're asleep.
Something feels wrong, something in your soul.
You feel heavy as if you're about to explode.
Your eyes begin to water,
but you begin to chant, that "I love you, Father."
The father that you have is always here.
He begins to speak to you loud and clear.
He said that, "if you call and believe in My name,
nothing will ever be the same."

The road that you once traveled
is hard, dusty, and full of gravel.
He was pierced in His side,
and all of our sins died.
From our Father, he was sent
so that all we need to do is to believe and repent.
For we're here on this earth for only a short time,
do you want to leave here, or do you want to be left behind?
We look at the world, but our eyes are closed.
The unsaved one doesn't want you
to see; he doesn't want to be exposed.

Beach by The Sea

As I walk on the beach by the sea, the winds
start to blow a bitterly cold.
I ask my Lord, "Why you have forsaken me?"
as I walk on the beach by the sea.
I suddenly hear a noise coming from the jungle.
I tried to run, but then I stumbled.
As I walk on the beach by the sea,
a deep fear swelled deep down inside.
I wanted to run, I wanted to hide.
As I walk on the beach by the sea,
I tried to yell, I tried to scream.
I wondered, will I wake up, is this all a dream?
As I walk on the beach by the sea,
all of a sudden, I was pouring wet.
I wondered, was this the sea or was it just sweat?

As I walk on the beach by the sea,
I yelled, "My Lord, why have you forsaken me?"
As I walk on the beach by the sea,
I saw a friend fall to the ground.
I called his name, but there was no sound.
As I walk on the beach by the sea,
I looked around to see all that I could see,
but all that I could see were bullets flying by me.
As I walk on the beach by the sea,
I felt a sizzling heat burning from deep inside.
I wondered, is this it, have I too died?
As I walk on the beach by the sea,
I feel as if I'm all alone,
without any device or phone to call home.
As I walk on the beach by the sea,
once again, the winds started to blow.

Where do they come from, I do not know.
As I walk on the beach by the sea,
my feet were stuck in the pavement,
as if I was planted in cement.
As I walk on the beach by the sea,
I told my home boy that I didn't want to go,
but I couldn't turn him down, I couldn't say no.
As I walk on the beach by the sea,
he told me that it would be a lot of fun.
He said that we would be the only ones with guns.
As I walk on the beach by the sea,
now all I heard was *pop, pop, pop.*
And then all of a sudden, I saw him drop.
As I walk on the beach by the sea,
I hear a voice telling me that this does not have to be,
if I would simply choose to not walk on the beach by the sea.

The Sunset

As the sun began to set,
you can be assured, you can truly bet,
that as the snow starts to appear on top,
the river that once flowed strong starts to drop;
as the tree that once stood straight and tall,
it now bends over, and sometimes it even falls;
as the grass that was once plush and green,
it is now thin, and some bald spots are even seen;
as the wind that once blew and didn't leave a trace,
now it only blows at a very slow pace.
Man is only here for a very short time.
When he's gone, what is it he'll leave behind?
He was once standing tall, he was king of the hill,
but now he only survives by taking lots of pills.

Man was not meant to live his life this way.
He was meant to live by his words, the words that he often should say.

As I Lay

When I look over and say good night,
I lay there and rest without any fright.
When I lay in bed at night and dream,
the world isn't so sad, so it might seem.
I lay there in my bed without any cares,
without any worries, without any nightmares.
All of the crying and sadness in the world has ceased
as I lay in my bed sleeping there in peace.
As I lay in bed with your body next to mine,
there's not a care in the world, none that I can find.
If there is any noise to be found,
I can use my pillow to block out any sound.
Lying on this mattress feels so good.
I would lie here all day if I could.

In this bed is where I want to stay.
I feel so at peace next to you as I lay.

Photo by Ryle's Photography

Author Paul Jones was born in Pine Bluff Arkansas, now resides in Fort Smith Arkansas. Although born and raised in the South, his experiences have taken him as far as California, Germany, and Honduras, to name a few. He has over fourteen years in the United States Armed Forces, as well as twenty-three years in law enforcement. As a law enforcement officer, he has served as a member of SWAT, bike patrol, and school resource and a director of security for a local high school. He is a member of Alpha Phi Alpha Fraternity Inc. Delta Sigma Lambda chapter. He has a Bachelor's Degree in Criminal Justice from American Intercontinental University, where he graduated Summa Cum Laude. He has other books to his credit: *Waking Up, Life and Love*, and *Living Life Poems to Live By*. Paul has also received many awards.

Printed in the United States
by Baker & Taylor Publisher Services